For Heidi and Simone
—M.R.

For my dad
—A.J.

Balzer + Bray is an imprint of HarperCollins Publishers.

Maryam Mirzakhani, Mathematician
Text copyright © 2021 by Megan Reid
Illustrations copyright © 2021 by Aaliya Jaleel
All rights reserved. Manufactured in Italy.

www.harpercollinschildrens.com

ISBN 978-0-06-291596-2

The artist used Procreate to create the digital illustrations for this book.
Typography by Dana Fritts

22 23 24 RTLO 10 9 8 7 6 5 4 3 2
❖
First Edition

MARYAM'S MAGIC

The Story of Mathematician Maryam Mirzakhani

By
MEGAN REID

Illustrations by
AALIYA JALEEL

BALZER + BRAY
An Imprint of HarperCollinsPublishers

Maryam Mirzakhani was a storyteller.

Every night before she went to bed . . .
She would tell her sister tales of fierce adventurers,
brave tricksters, and wizards with powers beyond compare.
No matter what kind of trouble they got into, they used
their wits to find a solution.

Every day after school . . .
She and her best friend, Roya, would roam the
swoops and curves of her city's busy streets. Their
favorite block was crowded with bookstores, and
they spent long afternoons dreaming themselves
into the plots of their favorite stories.

And every weekend . . .

She spread long rolls of paper on her bedroom floor, then crouched in a ball to scribble and color the worlds she imagined. They were intricate and beautiful, each detail designed to make her favorite scenes shine.

Together, her art and stories made magic.

Maryam wanted to be a famous writer when she grew up. She loved her reading and art classes. During the war that tore her home country of Iran apart, girls and women hadn't been allowed to attend school with boys—or sometimes even at all. But after the war was over, politicians started new schools to allow girls' talents to grow. "You are part of a lucky generation," Maryam's mother told her.

But when it came time for math each day, Maryam felt the opposite of lucky.

Maryam was a storyteller. She was NOT a mathematician.

The numbers made her head spin! How could she care about something so pointless and cold? She would rather doodle and dream.

When Maryam was twelve, her teacher announced that they would be learning geometry, a new kind of math. Maryam sighed.

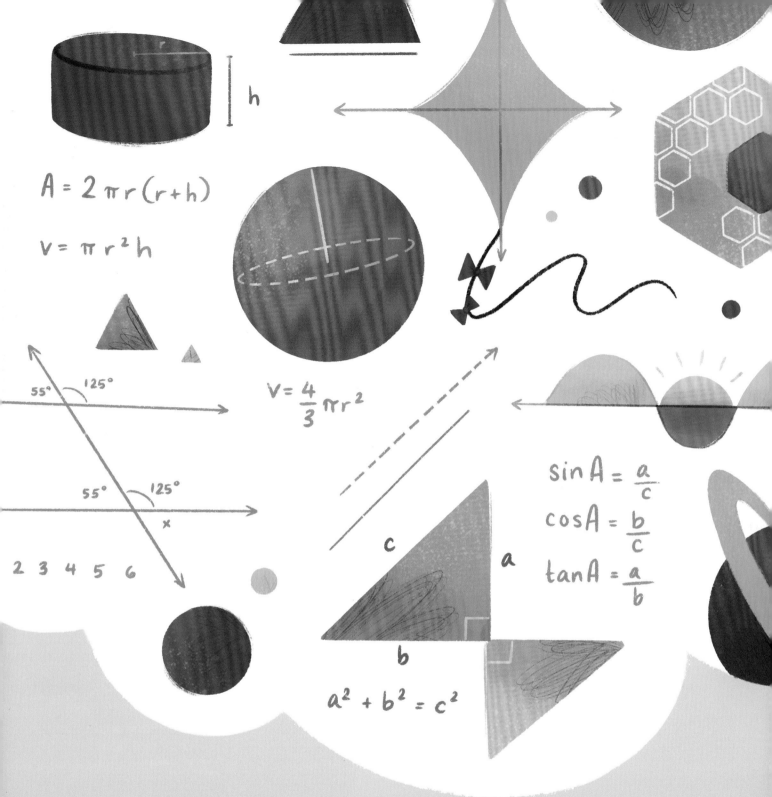

$$A = 2\pi r(r+h)$$

$$V = \pi r^2 h$$

$$V = \frac{4}{3}\pi r^2$$

55° 125°

55° 125°

x

2 3 4 5 6

$$\sin A = \frac{a}{c}$$

$$\cos A = \frac{b}{c}$$

$$\tan A = \frac{a}{b}$$

c

a

b

$$a^2 + b^2 = c^2$$

But geometry was different from any math she'd known before. Every number held a story. It made those numbers into shapes—and those shapes into pictures.

One degree of difference could make a triangle *acute* or *right*. Removing a Y shape from the end of a line showed that it was a segment, not a ray.

Maryam dreamed of magical shapes: they looked like bulging light bulbs and endless figure eights and layers and layers of doughnuts.

She made up fantastic tales about them. How many lines would it take to draw them? What kinds of patterns could cover them? If there were a hundred, or a thousand, or a BILLION shapes like them, could you tell the same stories about them all?

Maryam came to love these number stories like she loved the characters from her favorite books.

In high school, Maryam and Roya both entered the
International Mathematical Olympiad, a competition
for young mathematicians. They were the first girls
to make the Iranian team. That first year, they each
brought home a medal for their efforts. But it wasn't
the grand prize. Maryam and Roya wanted to be
heroines—the first girls to win first place for Iran!
Together, they trained long hours to prepare for the
next year's competition in Toronto, Canada.

When the judges announced the grand prize, Roya and the team cheered loudly. Maryam had gotten a perfect score!

Maryam was even more certain now that she wanted to devote her life to the stories numbers told. After college, she left Iran for graduate school at Harvard University in the United States.

She and her professors would talk about new formulas and theories in English for hours while she scribbled notes in Farsi, her native language.

When it was hard to solve a difficult equation, Maryam covered her house's floor with big sheets of paper and knelt to trace them with loops and lines, just as she had when she was young.

By now, Maryam was married with a child of her own. She drew so much that sometimes her daughter, Anahita, would tell people proudly that her mommy was a painter.

As she got older, Maryam's geometry stories
and pictures became more complex. She wanted
to stretch the limits of what humans understood
about the idea of infinity: equations that went on
and on without end.

She crafted mathematical formulas as if she were plotting the twists and turns of a suspenseful novel. "It's not only the question, but the way you try to solve it," she would tell her students.

Maryam began to write papers about her findings. Other thinkers would gather from far and wide to hear her speak.

For one tough problem, she imagined a twisty mirrored room where a thief was hiding. With the help of her pictures, math told her where a security guard would have to stand to protect valuable treasures.

People even called one of her discoveries "the magic wand theorem," because it worked like magic to solve many problems that scientists had been puzzling over for more than a hundred years. She explained it using the image of a pool table, with balls that zigged and zagged forever. If you covered the balls in paint, how long would it take for their scattered paths to color the table completely?

Maryam's magic wand math helped people all over the world. Astronauts could plot safer courses for their rocket ships. Meteorologists could predict weather patterns with more speed and accuracy. Doctors could understand how dangerous diseases grew and spread.

And in 2014, Maryam received an email from the International Mathematical Union telling her that she had won the Fields Medal, the most important award in math, for her magic wand.

She was the first woman and the first Iranian to ever receive the prize.

Maryam was proud, but not boastful. She just wanted to help others discover the amazing worlds math helped her see. She couldn't believe that, as a child, she very nearly gave up on it.

FIELDS MEDAL

Now even more people knew about her talent. But she had a secret that only her closest friends and family knew. Optimistic, curious Maryam was sick with breast cancer. For three years, she continued storytelling as the cancer spread to her liver, her bones.

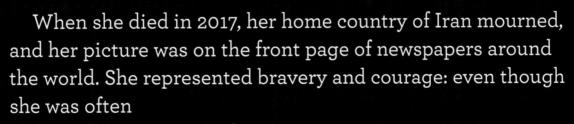

When she died in 2017, her home country of Iran mourned,
and her picture was on the front page of newspapers around
the world. She represented bravery and courage: even though
she was often

    the only woman in a classroom,
    the youngest to lead a research project,
    the smallest to speak in front of hundreds on a stage,
she never let that stop her from sharing the extraordinary
stories that numbers told.

PROFESSOR ROYA BEHESHTI
WASHINGTON UNIVERSITY IN ST. LOUIS

At Maryam's memorial, Roya, a math professor herself, spoke about her best friend. She told the story of a bright girl hungry for knowledge, who also had a kind heart and a beautiful mind.

She reminded the crowd that before Maryam was a mathematician, she was a storyteller.

But magically . . . she was always meant to be both.

Author's Note

I first heard about Maryam and her magic wand theorem in her *New York Times* obituary after she died in 2017. When I saw that Maryam was the first woman to win the most prestigious prize in mathematics, it felt shocking that that barrier had only recently been broken—in 2014! Sometimes it's difficult for me to wrap my head around the fact that there are still "firsts" for women to achieve, even though we know that talent, intelligence, and strength are qualities any person can possess.

I was sad that I had learned about this heroic figure only after she had passed away. I wished I could have let her know how much I admired her. But I was enchanted by a tidbit near the end of the article: "Dr. Mirzakhani often dived into her math research by doodling on vast pieces of paper . . . with equations at the edges." How exciting that a brilliant mathematician was also an artist, who could bring the secrets of the infinite universe down to her living room floor. When I did more research and learned that young Maryam actually disliked math as a child and tried to give up on it, I was even more surprised.

It reminded me uncomfortably of myself. I'm sure my teachers got tired of my whining about math! But one day a teacher overheard me complaining and handed me a play about algebra: *Arcadia* by Tom Stoppard. Reading it, I found math suddenly becoming real to me—and more than that, it became beautiful. I loved the idea that (along with lots of

hard work) art and stories gave Maryam the unique view of the world that catapulted her to the top of her field. She didn't have to give up or hide her other interests but instead transformed them into something important, brilliant, and groundbreaking.

I still get confused by more abstract ideas in math—trying to understand, and then figuring out ways to write about, Maryam's theorems was a challenge!—but it reminded me that none of us is just one thing. Maryam was a storyteller who was also a mathematics genius. Other people are sports stars who sing, or chefs who are computer whizzes, or firefighters with green thumbs. There are entire universes of talents and skills, and just because you love one thing dearly doesn't mean you can't excel at another. In fact, combining them might be the ingredient that helps you think, imagine, and achieve like no one else can.

I thought often of Maryam's daughter, Anahita, while writing this book, partly because Dr. Mirzakhani reminded me of my own mother, Michelle. She was also an immigrant to the United States who worked long hours to become a professor and researcher while raising my sister and me. I really believe that good moms are magicians in their own way. Above everything else, I hope that this version of Maryam's story captures even a little bit of what Anahita loved about her.

IMPORTANT DATES

1936 The first Fields Medal is awarded. Often called the Nobel Prize of mathematics (because there is no Nobel Prize for math), Fields Medals are awarded every four years to honor young mathematicians' achievements and support their future work.

MAY 12, 1977 Maryam Mirzakhani is born in Tehran, Iran.

1988 Maryam meets Roya Beheshti in middle school. The two girls sit together at a shared desk for the next seven years.

1990 According to Roya, Maryam becomes so frustrated with a math assignment that she rips it up and swears that she will never try to do better. Little does she know . . .

1994 Maryam travels to Hong Kong, where she competes in the International Mathematical Olympiad. She wins a gold medal but dreams of more.

1995 Maryam travels to Ontario, Canada, for the International Math Olympiad. At this competition, she wins a gold medal with a perfect score.

1995–1999 Maryam attends Sharif University, where she decides to devote her life to mathematics.

1999 Maryam moves to the United States to attend Harvard University for graduate school. (Luckily, Roya decides to attend MIT, just a few miles away.)

2004 Maryam finishes her PhD at Harvard University. Her dissertation is later called "a masterpiece" and "truly spectacular" by the mathematics community.

2004–2008 Maryam becomes a Clay Mathematics Institute Research Fellow and assistant professor at Princeton University.

2008 Maryam moves to Palo Alto, California, to become a professor of mathematics at Stanford University. She also marries Jan Vondrák, a fellow Stanford math professor and computer scientist from the Czech Republic.

2011 Maryam and Jan have a daughter, Anahita, who at three years old tells people that her mother is a painter.

2013 Maryam collaborates with Alex Eskin at the University of Chicago to publish a two-hundred-page paper that lays out the "magic wand theorem." That same year, she is diagnosed with breast cancer.

AUGUST 13, 2014 Maryam is the first woman (after fifty-two men) and the first Iranian to win the Fields Medal in mathematics for "her outstanding contributions to the dynamics and geometry of Reimann surfaces and their moduli spaces."

JULY 14, 2017 Maryam dies of metastatic breast cancer at the age of forty.

JULY 16–17, 2017 Iranian state-run newspapers break the country's rules about women being covered in public to show Maryam with her hair uncovered in her obituary: a rare honor. Iran's president, Hassan Rouhani, calls her an "eminent Iranian," and California Representative Jerry McNerney speaks to the US Senate, offering a tribute to Maryam and her pioneering work.

TO LEARN MORE ABOUT MARYAM AND HER WORK:

Barcelo, Hélène, and Stephen Kennedy. "Maryam Mirzakhani: 1977–2017." *Notices of the American Mathematical Society*, November 2018.

Chang, Kenneth. "Maryam Mirzakhani, Only Woman to Win a Fields Medal, Dies at 40." *New York Times*, July 16, 2017.

Halpern, Paul. "Maryam Mirzakhani, A Candle Illuminating the Dark." *Forbes*, August 1, 2017.

Klarreich, Erica. "A Tenacious Explorer of Abstract Surfaces." *Quanta* magazine, August 12, 2014.

Myers, Andrew, and Bjorn Carey. "Maryam Mirzakhani, Stanford Mathematician and Fields Medal Winner, Dies." *Stanford News*, July 15, 2017.

Zorich, Anton. "The Magic Wand Theorem of A. Eskin and M. Mirzakhani (trans: "Le théorème de la baguette magique de A. Eskin et M. Mirzakhani")." *Gazette des Mathématiciens* 142, 2014.

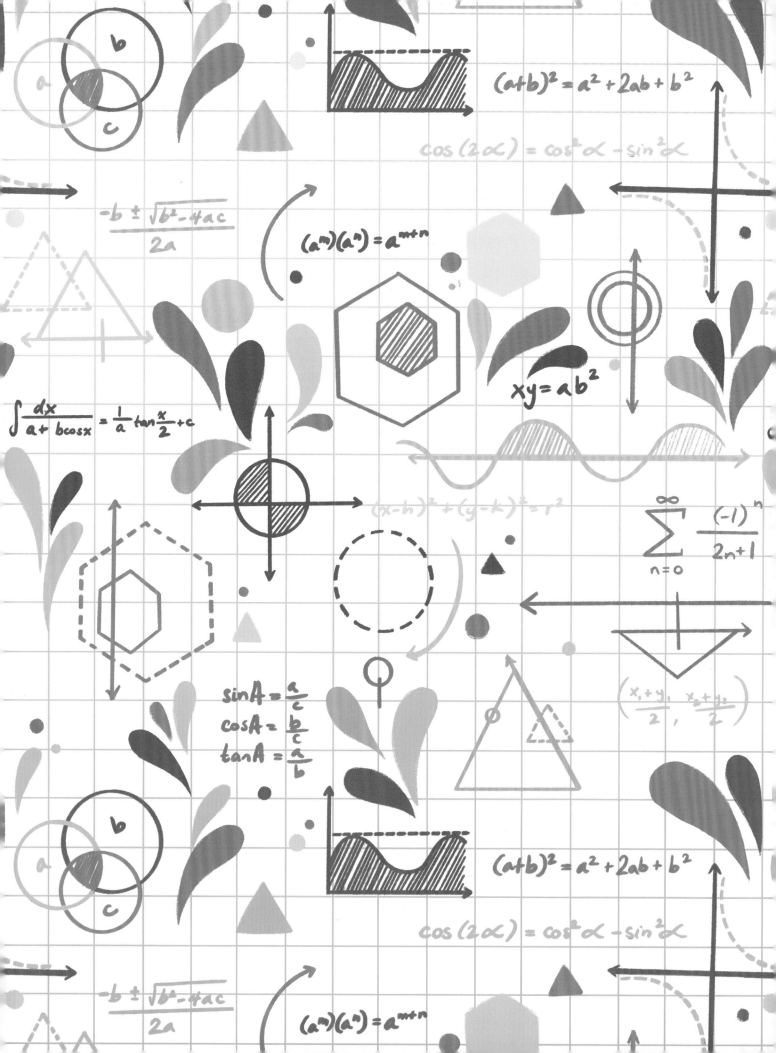